D1761387

decorative

needle felting

projects

Discover the relaxing art of needle felting and create 20 seasonal projects for the home

90710 000 518 631

decorative
needle felting
projects

**Discover the relaxing art of needle felting and
create 20 seasonal projects for the home**

GRETEL PARKER

Photographs by Jesse Wild & Gretel Parker

WHITE OWL

This book is dedicated with love and thanks to all my wonderful friends, followers and supporters around the world, who keep me going with their kind encouragement.

First published in Great Britain in 2022 by
PEN & SWORD WHITE OWL
An imprint of Pen & Sword Books Ltd
Yorkshire – Philadelphia

Copyright © Gretel Parker, 2022
@gretelparker

ISBN 9781399000307

The right of Gretel Parker to be identified as Author of this work has been asserted by her in accordance with the Copyright, Designs and Patents Act 1988.

A CIP catalogue record for this book is available from the British Library.

All rights reserved. No part of this book may be reproduced or transmitted in any form or by any means, electronic or mechanical including photocopying, recording or by any information storage and retrieval system, without permission from the Publisher in writing.

Group Publisher: Jonathan Wright
Series Editor and Publishing Consultant: Katherine Raderecht
Art Director: Jane Toft
Editor: Katherine Raderecht
Photography: Jesse Wild and Gretel Parker

Printed and bound in the UK, by Short Run Press Limited, Exeter.

Pen & Sword Books Ltd incorporates the Imprints of Pen & Sword Books
Pen & Sword Books Limited incorporates the imprints of Atlas, Archaeology, Aviation, Discovery, Family History, Fiction, History, Maritime, Military, Military Classics, Politics, Select, Transport, True Crime, Air World, Frontline Publishing, Leo Cooper, Remember When, Seaforth Publishing, The Praetorian Press, Wharncliffe Local History, Wharncliffe Transport, Wharncliffe True Crime and White Owl.

For a complete list of Pen & Sword titles please contact:
PEN & SWORD BOOKS LIMITED
47 Church Street, Barnsley, South Yorkshire S70 2AS, England
E-mail: enquiries@pen-and-sword.co.uk
Website: www.pen-and-sword.co.uk
or
PEN AND SWORD BOOKS
1950 Lawrence Rd, Havertown, PA 19083, USA
E-mail: Uspen-and-sword@casematepublishers.com
Website: www.penandswordbooks.com

DISCARDED FROM RICHMOND UPON THAMES LIBRARY SERVICE

LONDON BOROUGH OF RICHMOND UPON THAMES	
90710 000 518 631	
Askews & Holts	24-Jun-2022
746.046 PAR	
RTWH	

contents

introduction

Needle felting is the simple process of transforming wool into 3D objects using a barbed needle. It's a fun and relaxing craft that is much easier than it looks and gets amazing results. With just a few basic tools and straight forward needle felting techniques, you'll soon be on your way to making your own adorable felted creations.

Needle felting has been my passion since February 2008, when I first picked up a felting needle and, after some tentative poking, shaped a piece of rough wool into a little brown bunny. Back then, needle felting was still relatively unknown in the U.K. and, as an early adopter of the craft, I eagerly shared my creations and new skills on my blog, 'Middle of Nowhere'. I subsequently opened an Etsy shop and sold my woolly creatures all over the world. Later, I began writing my own patterns and sharing my particular method of needle felting with others.

The simplicity of using a single barbed needle and a piece of unspun wool to sculpt whatever comes out of my imagination remains a wondrous thing. I also find the repetitive motion of using the needle relaxing and calming. Since those early days, I have seen needle felting thrive and grow into a mainstream craft. Alongside that, my own work has also developed as I continue to explore the possibilities of design and style using the endlessly versatile medium of wool.

This book is a celebration of using various haberdashery materials to embellish and adorn home needle felted decorations and wearables throughout the seasons. It also showcases techniques that I hope will inspire you to create your own beautiful needle felting and to continue to experiment with the many ways you can enhance your projects.

Including clear step-by-step photos and instructions, the patterns are easy to follow, even for complete beginners. No previous needle felting experience is needed!

basic tools

One of the many joys of needle felting is that getting started is simple and affordable. All you need to get going are a few pieces of wool roving (unstructured, unspun wool used in various crafts such as needle felting), felting needles and a felting mat - that's it! From this basic kit, as you continue with your needle felting journey, it's just a matter of building up your stock of roving - almost like a woolly paintbox - and adding to your stash of sewing threads, textile scraps and beads.

WOOLS

I use merino wool roving exclusively for my work and designs; the fine fibres enable me to get a beautifully smooth finish and there is a larger choice of colours available on the market. You can, of course, use any kind of wool for these patterns, but the result may be a little more 'hairy' and rough than if you use merino wool. If you are just starting out and don't know where to start with colours, than I recommend buying a selection of small amounts of around 15-25g or a multi-pack containing a good variety of shades.

TOOLS

When you are starting out, a felting mat or sponge, to protect you from the sharp needle point as you are working, is a must. The cheapest entry-level mat is a dense sponge block, which will last for enough time until you decide to invest in a more durable one. These sponge blocks can be bought from specialist fibre suppliers, or you can use a piece of upholstery foam.

A bristle brush will last for years and is my preferred work base. They can be made of plastic or wood, such as the ones shown in this book. If you find your work is sticking to the bristles, cover your brush with a smooth, durable cloth to take the impact of your needle.

FELTING NEEDLES

A felting needle has a thin, shaped steel shaft with a latch at one end to keep it in a holder (if you are using one) and several tiny, sharp barbs running partway from the mid-length to the tip. If you hold a needle up to the light and look closely you can see the shape of the shaft and the barbs which mesh the wool fibres together as you work.

What type of needle and how many to use can be as individual to the needle felt crafter as a pencil is to an artist. The size of the shaft ranges from 42 (very fine) to 36 (thick), getting larger as the number goes down. I never use anything below size 40, as merino wool is so fine that a heavier needle is less effective at meshing the fibres together. My rule of thumb is to use a size 40 needle to start your work off with and a size 42 for finishing off and smoothing the surface.

There are several different shaft shapes but I only use two types in my work: triangular and spiral. Triangular needles are the workhorse of the needle felting world and, if you want to keep things simple, I suggest just using them in sizes 40 and 42 for your work. Spiral (or twisted) needles are lovely to use and will glide in and out of the wool smoothly; I often use just a single size 40 spiral needle for a project, from start to finish.

You may find you break a few needle tips when you start needle felting - this is quite

Clover long lasting, needle felting bristle mat with a plastic base

Dimensions 'Feltworks' long lasting, felting bristle mat with wooden base

1. Clover pen style multi-needle holder 2. Turned wood needle storage case 3. Church Mouse pen-style single needle holder 4. Damp proof plastic needle storage tube 5. Universal budget foam felting mat

basic tools

normal. Breakages are usually down to the action of your hand as you work – the needle should be going in and out of the wool without force and never into the felting mat, which is where it can get caught and snap. Finally, felting needles are very sharp, so use them carefully or consider investing in some finger guards.

NEEDLE HOLDERS

While many people prefer to use a felting needle in their hand, there are good reasons to use a needle holder, especially if you are just starting out. A holder will reduce strain on your wrist. I like to use a longer, pen style holder, as it is slim and allows for flexibility of movement. If you want to try experimenting with using more than one needle, then go for a multi needle holder which can be useful for larger projects. You don't have to worry about buying the right sized needle for the holder because they are generic and designed so that the latch at the top slots into the holder whatever size they are.

SEWING NEEDLES AND TOOLS
Needles
Short needles for small patches and darns
Long needles for lines of stitching
Beading needles - these are ultra-thin, and very useful for attaching tiny seed beads
Extra tools - small sharp scissors, a sewing awl, pins, needle threader

THREADS

Any kind of thread or wool yarn, even thin cotton sewing thread, can be used for adding decoration to your needle felt projects. I use a variety of threads in my work so that I have a good choice of thickness's and finishes. Perle, DMC, thin tapestry yarn, new and vintage silks, rayons and my favourite, Danish Flower thread; all can be used to add colour, dimension and balance to a design. When planning your embellishment, think about the weight and thickness of the thread you are using; a small darn made from a thicker Perle thread will have a dense, chunky appearance as opposed to a larger but more delicate one sewn with a thinner, cotton thread, so get creative by experimenting and mixing them up.

NEEDLE FELT BASICS

Needle felting is essentially sculpting with unspun wool, using a sharp felting needle to mould and mesh the wool fibres together. Although needle felt artists often refer to their technique as 'stabbing', it is more effective to use a gentle jab. Being heavy handed with your needle won't necessarily make your project come together more quickly, so when you begin a pattern, just use a regular, rhythmic up and down action, inserting the needle into the wool but not the felting mat (this can lead to needle breakage). Turning your work is essential, to keep it three dimensional. It is also important to work all over the surface to retain the same density.

My way of working is to felt very firmly, as I like my pieces to be long lasting and I find it easier to embellish a clean, sturdy form. However, you may find that you prefer a looser, more 'fluffy' finish. As you experiment more, you'll find your own style and how you want your work to look.

following the patterns

Many of my patterns begin with 'take a length of wool', which means wool roving. Generally speaking, the average width of wool roving is 5-7cm, but this can vary. So if you have a piece of roving that is wider than the pattern suggests, thin it down by splitting it vertically (lengthwise) or add more if it isn't quite wide enough.

The patterns are more about process rather than exact measurements. Measurements are primarily there to keep the project roughly to the scale of the design shown. It can be tricky to measure roving precisely as it has loose, wispy ends, but don't worry - so long as the length is as close as possible to what I advise, your piece should end up the right size.

It can be tempting to cut your wool, to ensure you have a precise length, however I try to avoid this because sharp, cut ends of wool are more difficult to work in than ragged torn ends which will blend in more easily. I've designed the projects to show an easy to follow step method which you can enlarge or reduce by altering the amounts of wool you use. Wool is very forgiving, so if you do feel you have wandered from the design shown, just add or take away whatever needs fixing and patch over any obvious mends.

Where extra elements are required, such as darning or patching, the pattern will refer you back to the corresponding technique page, should you need it.

If you are new to needle felting, many of the patterns such as My Mended Heart Garland (see page 24) or the Easter Jewel Eggs (see page 36) are a good starting point, to give you a feel for the wool and how it firms up as you work it.

Finally, have fun, experiment with the different techniques and enjoy your new favourite hobby!

techniques

LAYERING WOOL FOR FINISHING OFF

I use a technique that I call 'layering' which finishes off the surface smoothly once the piece is shaped and firmed. This prepares the piece for embellishment and covers any lumps and bumps. You can add more layers to neaten it up further if you feel you need to. Work closely and shallowly with the needle tip, to get an even texture. I layer my work with several small patches of wool rather than trying to cover a piece all in one go, as makes it easier to control.

1. Use small amounts of wool that have been thinned out to an even gauze; you should be able to see your fingers through it. The fibres should be lying straight and as tidily as possible.

2. Apply these small patches of wool neatly all over all your work, following the line of the design and keeping the fibres flowing in the same direction where possible.

3. Use the tip of a needle to smooth out any irregularities, working closely and not too deeply.

4. If you have excess fibres which make your piece look a bit 'hairy' you can trim them away by holding sharp scissors flat against the surface and very carefully shearing them off.

techniques

STITCHING ONTO FELT

While this is primarily a book about needle felting, I have used very basic sewing techniques in some of the patterns, but these are very easy to do, even if you are a novice sewer. You will find that a simple running stitch, a few random seed stitches or regularly placed individual straight stitches are a very effective way of adding surface patterns to your work. Your wool should be very firm when stitching onto it, so that the threads don't sink into your project.

1. Make a little dent into the project with a sharp point, so that the knot vanishes into the felt. You can use a sewing awl or sewing scissors for this.

2. Tie a small knot on the end of the thread and pull the needle into the wool, away from your start point. Cover the dent and knot with a scraping of surface wool if they show through.

3. Pull the thread through and begin your stitching. Your stitches should sit gently but snugly on the wool surface; try not to pull the thread too tightly.

4. When you are finished, bring the thread out away from the end point, pull it taut and snip it off, so that the thread end disappears back into the body of the felt.

techniques

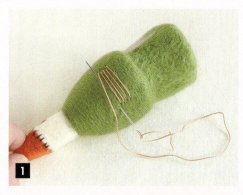 

DARNING ONTO FELT

Decorative darning is a fabulous way of embellishing a piece of needle felt. Make sure that it is worked very firmly and is as smooth as you can make it, so that the threads sit on the surface and don't catch too many stray fibres. Darning onto felt is very similar to mending a household item such as socks (but more enjoyable, in my opinion!). I use a medium sized needle with a decent sized hole and a good length of embroidery thread so that I can complete the darn in one go.

1. Ensuring that the knot of the thread is brought away from your start point, stitch a row of horizontal length stitches. Your tension should be taut but not too tight.

2. Use the blunt end of the needle to weave under and over the horizontal threads. Take the thread back under the darn to the opposite side for accuracy of placement.

3. As there is some 'give' in felted wool, I slightly overestimate where the thread goes in and comes out, as it will fractionally sink into your work and decrease in length.

4. If you run out of thread, just use another length. When the darn is complete, bring the thread out away from the work area, gently pull it taut and snip it off neatly.

techniques

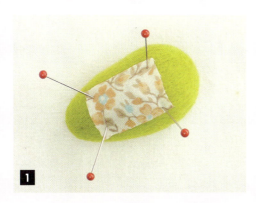

PATCHING ONTO FELT

Tiny patches are an adorable addition to any piece of work and are so easy to do. If you have any treasured but fragile scraps of material, this is the perfect way to preserve them. Cotton sewing thread in a contrasting colour to the felt and fabric will stand out visually, as will using a thicker single strand thread such as Perle or Danish Flower thread.

Use a small needle, so you can manipulate it easily. Don't worry if your stitches look a little wonky, as this is part of the naïve charm. The felt should be very firm, so that the thread doesn't sink into the wool. There will be some 'give' as you sew, but with practise you will be able to gauge how big to make a stitch so it shows up clearly.

1. Carefully cut your patch out, using small, sharp scissors and anchor it over the felt using a pin in each corner to keep it snug to the surface while you are sewing.

2. Use a knotted thread and pull the knot into the felt, before stitching around the edge of the patch. I like to use very simple stitches which aren't too neat and tidy.

3. Remove each pin as you go along. When you have sewn all around the edge of the patch, take the thread out away from the patch, pull the thread taut and snip it off.

15

techniques

BEADING ONTO FELT Seed beads are fabulous for adding tiny, instant pops of colour. You can use standard seed beads or if, like me, you are very particular about uniformity and roundness, Toho and Miyuki beads. Seed beads come in various sizes, the most common ones being 6/0 (large), 8/0, 11/0 and 15/0 (tiny). For these projects I have used mainly 11/0 beads, as they are a good medium size. The colours and finishes you choose are entirely a matter of personal taste; my own preference is for flat, opaque colours that stand out against the wool, but there are hundreds of different options to explore.

Seed beads can usually be sewn with a normal, thin needle if they are 11/0 or larger. If you are using the smaller 15/0 beads, you will find a skinny beading needle essential. Use a very long length of cotton that matches the colour of the bead as closely as possible, or invisible thread if you are using clear beads.

As with stitching and patching, knot the end of the thread and take the needle into the wool away from your start point. When finished, take the thread out away from the final bead - I take it in and out of the wool a few times first, just for extra security, before snipping off.

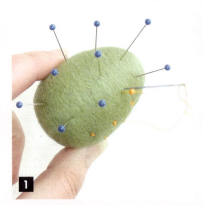

SCATTERED BEADS

I love a pretty 'ditzy' pattern. To ensure an even distance between beads, I use glass headed place pins as markers. A sewing awl or sharp scissors can be used to make tiny dents for the beads, so that they snuggle into the wool.

1. Lay out a few pins so that they are scattered equidistant apart and stitch the first beads in. For an even finish, use a sharp point to make a little dent for each bead to sit in.

2. After you have attached the first beads, move the pins into the next few places, using your eye to judge the best place for each one.

3. Continue like this until you have covered the area that you are decorating.

techniques

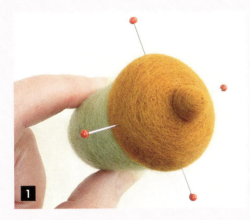

UNIFORM PATTERNS

This method works if you prefer an orderly placement of your beads and also works well with rounder, more symmetrical shapes, such as eggs. These steps are for a simple layout of eight points, but if you want a more closely packed pattern, you can add extra pins in between the original eight. Again, use a sharp point to make indentations in the wool for the beads to nestle into as you work.

1. Lay the first four pins out like compass points, one at North, the next opposite at South, then East and West, so that your piece is divided into quarters.

2. Pin out the other four points in between, taking care to place them centrally and keeping them in line. Now you have eight evenly spaced pins where your beads will go.

3. Remove each pin as you sew a bead in. When you have completed a full circuit, mark out the next line. Repeat until finished, decreasing the number of beads as the shape narrows.

techniques

SEWING IN EYES Although it is perfectly possibly to needle felt little eyes, I prefer to use glass beads or traditional toy eyes, as they have a lifelike sparkle to them. You can use seed beads or black onyx beads which come in a variety of sizes from 2mm upwards if you want consistent roundness. Use a strong black thread for security, so that the eyes don't fall out.

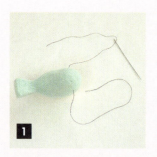 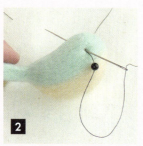 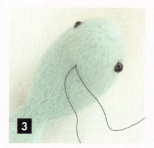 

SIDEWAYS METHOD

1. Take the thread through the head, from one side to the other, where the eyes are to be positioned. Make sure the sides are equal and remove the needle from the thread.

2. Put a bead onto one of the threads and rethread the needle. Take the needle into the eye area, bringing it out at the back of the head. Pull the thread and bead snugly into the wool.

3. Repeat this on the other side, bringing the second thread out at the same place as the first thread, at the back of the head. Un-thread the needle.

4. Knot the threads, making sure the beads are firm in the wool. Rethread the needle with all the ends and bring out at a point away from the knot. Snip off.

 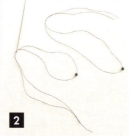  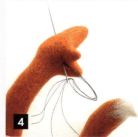

FRONT METHOD

1. Use a sewing awl or the points of small, sharp scissors to drill into the wool, creating sockets into which the beads can nestle.

2. Thread each bead separately onto two good lengths of strong black thread, then take the first one and thread the loose ends onto a good sized needle.

3. Take the needle into the socket and out at the back of the head, pulling the bead snug. Repeat with the second bead, bringing the ends out at the same point.

4. Knot all the ends together so that the beads are well secured in the wool and bring the thread ends out away from the knot before snipping off.

techniques

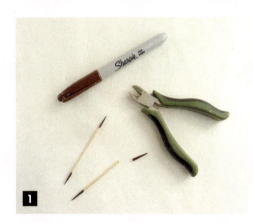

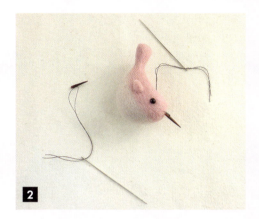

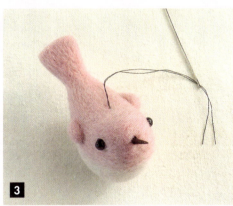

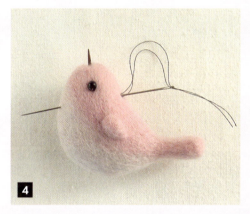

MAKING TINY BEAKS

Little wooden beaks add to the toy-like charm of a bird, although they can of course be needle felted, as in the Chirpy Chicken Bowl pattern (see page 32). Cocktail sticks and kebab skewers are perfect for beaks and can be left natural or coloured using a metallic gold pen or Sharpie, depending on the effect you want.

1. Colour both ends (which will give you two beaks) and leave to dry. Then cut them off using plier cutters - leave a small amount of excess wood which will disappear into the bird head.

2. Tie a good length of strong cotton thread around the cut end. Drill a fairly deep hole into the beak area, thread both loose ends onto a needle and take them into the little cavity you've made, pulling the beak into the head

3. Bring the threads out at the back of the head, removing the needle and knotting them together tightly.

4. Re-thread the needle and bring the loose ends out away from the knot, snipping them off neatly.

techniques

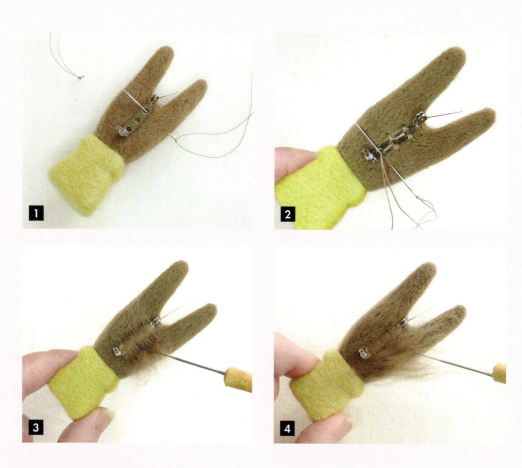

ATTACHING A BROOCH BACK

If you are planning on wearing a brooch regularly, it's a good idea to make sure that the metal pin is fixed well onto the felt. This method of stitching and then over-felting will keep it in place with no wobbling.

1. Use strong thread that matches the colour of the wool. It should have a small knot in the end. Take the thread into the wool away from the pin and bring the needle up into the brooch bar.

2. Stitch the pin firmly onto the back of the brooch with strong thread; the felt has to be firmly felted so that it will not sink into the wool.

3. Use a short tuft of wool and arrange it across the stitched brooch bar, needling it down on either side of the metal.

4. Take two more short tufts of wool and needle them over each side of the brooch bar, across the first band of wool, working them down so that they blend into the felt underneath.

techniques

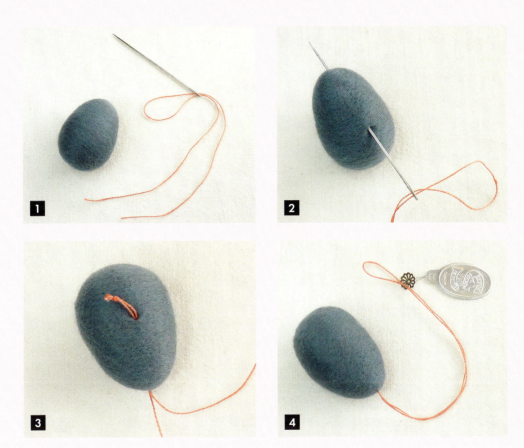

ADDING A DANGLE

Adding a loop of thread or floss instantly turns a hand-crafted treasure into a beautiful ornament. A small jewellery maker's bead cap can be added for extra decoration. If you are making a collection of dangles, measure out equal amounts of thread before inserting them, so that they all hang at a similar length.

1. To make a tidy loop for a dangling ornament, use a good length of doubled over embroidery floss, threaded onto a medium to long needle with the looped end going through the eye.

2. Drill a little hole in the felt, using a sewing awl or sharp scissors, and take the thread into the felt and up to the top of the piece, leaving the loose thread ends outside.

3. Knot the ends of the thread together and gently pull them into the felt, so that it disappears. If the area is untidy, neaten it up with a tiny patch of wool.

4. Jewellery caps add a lovely finishing touch. Use a needle threader to pull the loop top through the cap hole and down to the piece to nestle it on top of the felt.

chapter one: spring

As we emerge out of winter darkness, lighten up your colour palette with fresh greens and soft pastels. Add some cute fun to your wardrobe with a sweet bunny pops brooch, adorn a wall with a pretty heart garland and create stylish decorated eggs for your Easter tree, with adorable love birds nestling in the branches; and don't forget a chirpy chicken bowl for displaying chocolate treats.

my mended heart garland

These folk art inspired hearts are super quick and easy to make. I've chosen a selection of subdued colours with a couple of brights for highlights and colour matched the darning threads to bring them all together.

Difficulty - easy

You will need
For each heart (finished size approximately 8cm in length)

- A selection of wools in the colours of your choice - about 25cm max for each heart

- Size 40 or size 42 felting needle (triangular or spiral)

- A felting mat

- 1 metre of 15mm ribbon or tape - brown linen ribbon used here

- Various darning threads to match and complement your colour scheme - Danish Flower threads used here

- Needle and strong thread for stitching the garland together

- Optional - small vintage curtain rings. Or you can simply knot a small loop at each end of the garland.

GRETEL'S TIPS

- This pattern uses a metre of ribbon for seven hearts, but this can be increased or decreased to alter the size of your garland.

- These hearts can also be used to make sweet little dangles (see page 21) or use a single one to make a jazzy brooch (see page 20).

25

1. Split a small length of roving vertically and use a length that measures about 20 x 3-4cm. Form it into a simple heart shape as shown above and begin working it on your felting mat.

2. Draw any excess wool from the edge into the middle, to bulk it up and then tuck the end fibres back into the heart.

3. Work both sides until you have a defined heart. These are folk art style hearts, so they don't have to be perfect; a little wonkiness will give them character.

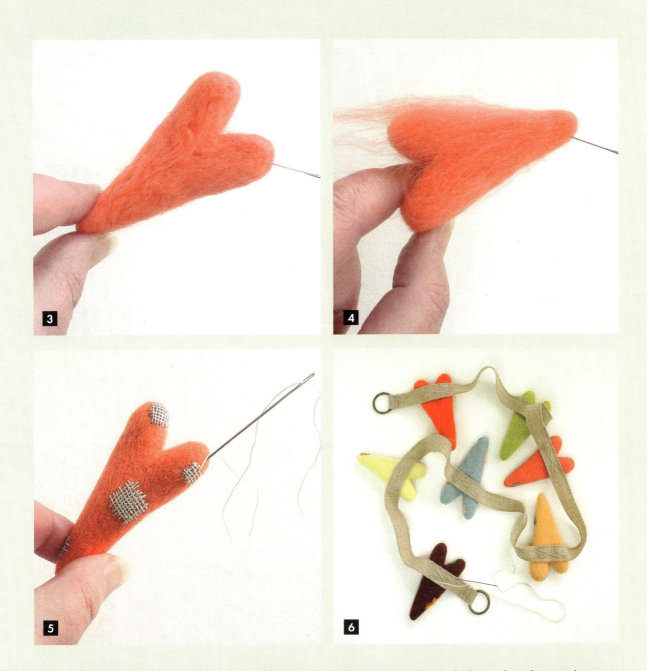

4. Cover the finished heart with a thin layer of wool (see page 12) until you have a smooth, firm finish. Make as many hearts as you need; just three will make a lovely mini garland.

5. Embellish the hearts with small, loosely woven

darns. I've used Danish Flower thread to match my colour scheme, but you can use any embroidery floss.

6. Sew the rings on the ribbon, before stitching each heart on at regular intervals. Use a single wide cross stitch to fix the ribbon close to the top of each heart.

bunny pops

With the arrival of warmer days, it's time to think about swapping your winter woolies for a lighter outfit, so why not make a darling Bunny Pop brooch to match? You can leave the jumper plain, or decorate it with a special, tiny vintage button or sweetly sentimental darns.

Difficulty - medium

You will need
For each Bunny Pop (finished size approximately 10cm tall)

- 20 - 25cm wool for the head, slivers of pink for the ear linings and a few cm of wool in the colour of your choice for the jumper

- Size 40 or size 42 felting needle (triangular or spiral)

- A felting mat

- Bead eyes - I've used 4mm black onyx beads

- Pink embroidery thread for the nose

- A needle and strong colour matched thread for sewing on the brooch back

- Optional decorations - seed beads, embroidery thread for tiny darns, a vintage button

29

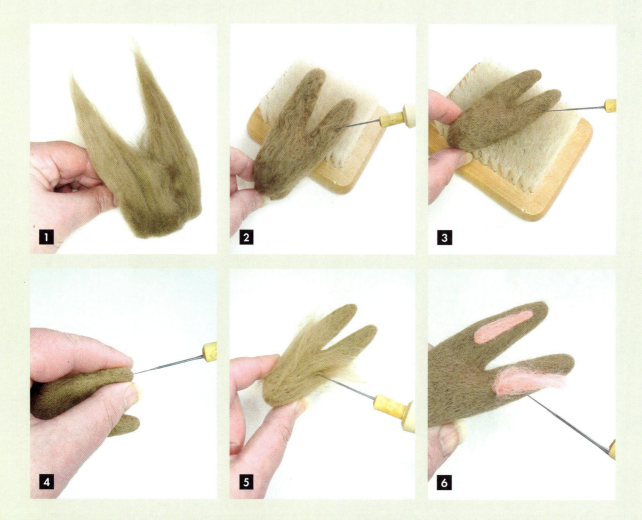

1. Take a length of wool measuring no more than 15cm. Fold it over and with the folded half at the bottom, divide the top portion of the fibres into two equal amounts for the ears.

2. Shape the wool into a simple rabbit head. The front should be slightly rounded and the back should be flat. Tuck any loose fibres over and back into your work.

3. If you work the front of the face directly on your felting mat, the back of the head will naturally become flat. If you remove it from time to time you will avoid the wool sticking.

4. Use your fingers to pinch the ears into shape as you needle, to get a nice point. You can even the sizes up by adding a little more wool, if needed.

5. Work the head until it is firm (especially the ears). Add thin layers of wool front and back to finish the surface off neatly (see page 12).

6. Use skinny slivers of wool to create the insides for the ears. Work carefully with the tip of your needle to get a clean neat outline.

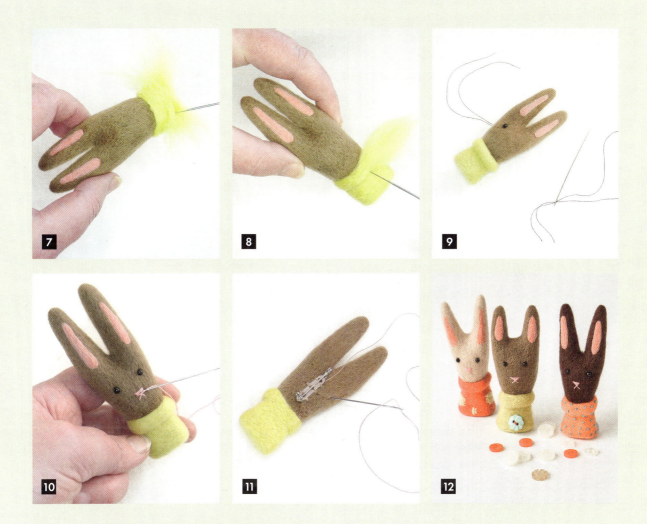

7. To make the jumper, needle small lengths of wool wrapped around the bottom of the head, making a gentle curve for the chin area. Keep the back flat, as you did with the head.

8. When the jumper is built up, add an extra short strip to the front to form a roll neck and when it's all looking nice, cover it with a thin layer of wool to finish it off (see page 12).

9. Sew in the eyes using the front facing method (see page 18) and tie the threads together at the back. If you don't have beads, use French knots sewn with black embroidery floss.

10. Sew a nose and mouth by stitching a little X and filling in the top part with a few tiny stitches, making a triangle to indicate the nose.

11. Attach a brooch pin to the back with strong thread, patching over with wool for extra strength (see page 20). I placed it vertically to carry the weight evenly.

12. Decorate the jumper with a pretty button, seed beads or darns, to give your bunny a unique character.

chirpy chicken bowls

The arrival of spring is such a joyous time of the year! It's lovely to feature friendly chickens in one form or another in your home to celebrate the lighter days. Using these measurements will give you a small, palm sized bowl, perfect for displaying little sweet eggs.

Difficulty - medium

You will need
For each bowl (finished size approximately 7-8cm in bowl width)

- Merino wool, approx 25cm, in chicken colour of choice and small scraps of wattle and beak colours

- Size 40 or size 42 felting needle (triangular or spiral)

- A felting mat

- 2x black seed beads or 2mm onyx beads

- Strong black thread and a needle

- Optional decorations - seed beads, fabric scraps for patches, embroidery threads for darns and stitches (Danish Flower threads and DMC Perle used here)

GRETEL'S TIPS

- If you want to make a larger bowl, follow the same instructions but simply increase the amount of wool you use.

- This method of working follows the same principle as making simple hand built clay coil pots - gradually increasing the size by winding a length of wool round and round itself while working, to create the vessel shape.

1. Take a length of roving 25cm long. Split it in half lengthwise, so that it is roughly 4cm in width. Put one of the pieces aside for now and keep the other to use immediately.

2. Begin by coiling one end of the roving around itself (like a snail shell) on the felting mat to make the base of the bowl, needling it into place to make a small, shallow spiral.

3. When the base is approximately 4-5cm across, carry on winding and needling, building up the height and thickness of the bowl wall.

4. As the wool becomes firmer, take it off the mat and work on both sides, firming up the bowl wall. Use the tip of the needle to distribute the wool evenly.

5. If you need to, use some of the second piece of wool to increase the height. Keep turning as you work to ensure an even roundness until it is 6cm across the top and 3-4cm in height.

6. Using a good pinch of wool, shape a tapering head, joining it to the bowl edge. You may want to add a bit more wool underneath to enlarge the chest.

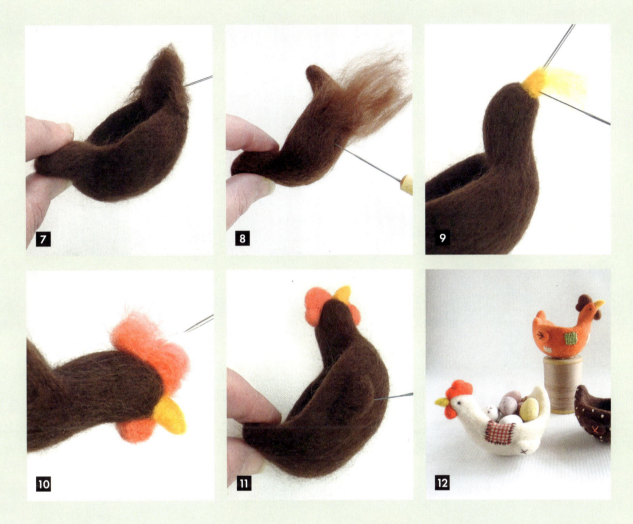

7. Add a perky tail using a good pinch of wool. Use the needle tip to sculpt a fancy scalloped end or keep it plain and simple.

8. Neaten up the surface with a thin layer of wool (see page 12) and work the chicken all over, so that you have a sturdy base ready for embellishment.

9. Add the beak by first inserting a spare needle at an angle. Wind a fragment of yellow wool around and up the shaft, needling until the beak is shaped. Remove the guide needle.

10. Bright wattles are worked directly onto the head, using scraps of wool and the tip of your needle to shape them, before adding the eyes using the sideways method (see page 18).

11. Use two equal small rolls of wool to add rain drop shaped wings directly to the bowl sides. I've added simple stitches in contrasting thread for a rustic country look.

12. Pretty up your chicken by adding seed beads (see page 16) for a speckled hen, or tiny darns (see page 14) or using gingham for patches (see page 15).

easter jewel eggs

Easter trees are growing in popularity, with egg decorations as the star feature. Display them on a small branch or twig for a natural, woodland effect so that they really stand out. This is the simplest of patterns and yet there is so much scope for beautiful colour and decoration, so let your creativity run wild!

Difficulty - easy

You will need
For each small egg (finished size approximately 5cm tall)

- Small amount of Merino wool, about 15 cm in total

- Size 40 or size 42 felting needle (triangular or spiral)

- A felting mat

- Decorations - seed beads, embroidery threads, tiny fabric scraps

- Needle for adding dangle loop and optional jewellery cap (8mm bronze flower cap used here)

- Matching threads for the dangle loops

GRETEL'S TIPS

- I've colour matched my eggs with the loop threads and finished off with a small decorative jewellery cap (see page 21) held in place with three or four tiny stitches.

- If you'd like to make larger eggs, just increase the amount of wool and follow the same process.

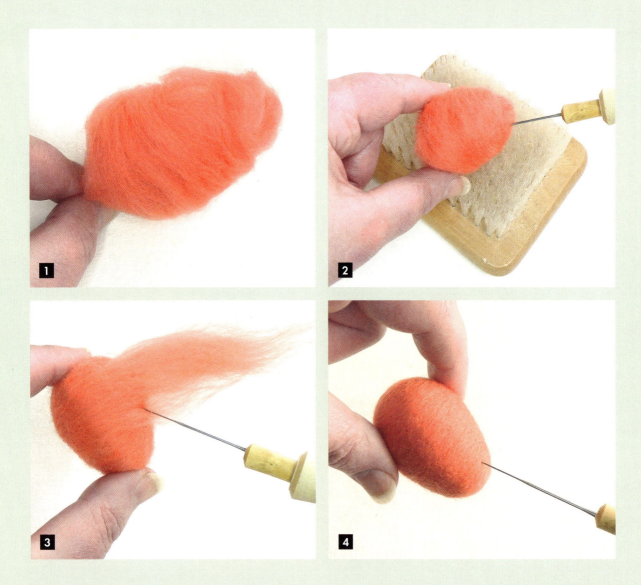

MAKING THE EGGS

1. Take a small amount of wool, approximately 10-12 cm, and gently roll it up. Arrange it so that you have a fat end for the bottom and a thinner end for the top of the egg.

2. Work it until it the wool thickens up, turning it as you work; this is important, as you want a nice rounded form. Add more thin layers, building the shape up gradually.

3. The largest part of the egg is around the middle, so you may want to add some thin strips of wool around the 'waist' to create a lovely balanced shape.

4. Your egg needs to be quite solid so that you can decorate it easily, so keep working it with small, even jabs until it really firms up and is ready for embellishment.

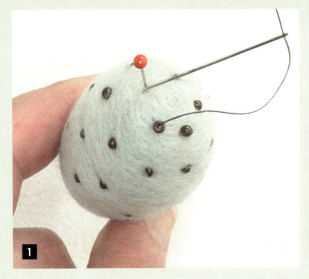

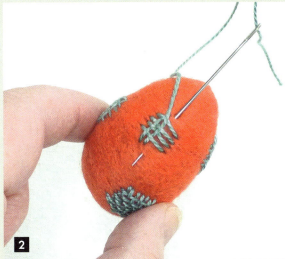

DECORATING YOUR EGGS (all sizes)

1. To get an evenly placed pattern of beads, use the compass method (see page 17). Larger beads will give a polka dot effect or use smaller ones for a sweet scattering of colour.

2. Add little darns around your egg (see page 14) Use just one as a statement embellishment or a few various sized ones. Try thinner or thicker sized threads for different effects.

3. Add miniature patches (see page 15). This is a lovely way to preserve those tiny fragments of gorgeous fabric that you can't bear to throw away.

4. Create stripes by using long stitches. Use the centre of each end as universal points for your needle so that the stripes begin and finish in the same place.

sweetie pie love birds

Inspired by kitsch vintage 1950's ornaments, these cheerful bundles of fluff are wired onto a natural twig and are made from a single core colour before extra colour is added. Here you can 'paint' with wool, using the tip of your felting needle to gently blend different colours into each other to resemble feathers.

Difficulty - easy

You will need
For each bird (finished size approximately 7-8cm in length)

- Merino wool, in a soft off-white or light fawn, about 25cm, small amounts of pastel colours of your choice to cover

- Size 40 or size 42 felting needle (triangular or spiral)

- A felting mat

- 1x cocktail stick beak (see p. 19) or you can simply needle felt one

- 2x large black beads or 4mm onyx beads

- Strong black thread and a needle

- Embroidery floss for decoration - Anchor Pearl Cotton, colour 54 used here

- Flexible wire to fix the bodies onto the twig - brown paper covered florist's wire used here

- A nice looking twig (trim off any untidy ends)

GRETEL'S TIP

- Display just one bird on a single cutting, or make a gorgeous vase arrangement with a little flock perched jauntily together.

1. Roll up a small piece of roving; this is just a core, so it doesn't have to be perfect. Shape it into a lopsided egg, with the fatter part being the head/tummy.

2. Wrap a large piece of wool around the core when it is shaped - I've used roughly 15cm. Needle it onto the core, following the same contours.

3. When the body is firmed up, add a layer of pastel wool, covering the back, head and top half of the

body, with a good overlap at the back, which you will use for the tail.

4. Needle the pastel wool well onto the body, then use the spare wool to form a little tail, spreading it out at the end to shape a fan. Tuck any loose ends underneath the tail tip.

5. Add a final thin layer of wool to the main colour (see page 12) and then a thin layer to the tummy. Use

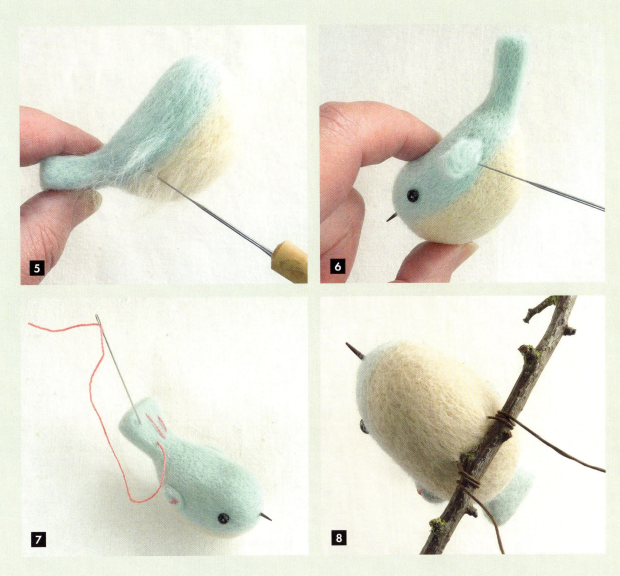

the needle tip to scrape and blur the edges together, creating a feathered effect.

6. Sew in the beak (see page 19) and eyes, using the sideways method (see page 18), then add tiny wings using two same sized pinches of wool. These are needled straight onto the body.

7. Add three long stitches to the tail, starting with a long middle one followed by two equal sized shorter ones on either side. Sew a cross stitch to each of the wings, for a touch of homespun charm.

8. Insert a good length of wire through your bird's tummy and, after careful positioning, wind each piece around the twig several times, as neatly as possible, snipping off any excess to create feet.

chapter two: summer

Relax in the cool shade with these gentle needle felt projects; a gorgeous rose wrist wrap to wear at Midsummer parties, table decorations of luscious decorative strawberries and playful lollipop trees. Create your own rural hideaway with an egg cup hill landscape, and pep up a plain tee shirt with the pop of a bright ladybird brooch.

egg cup hill

One of my favourite eras of graphic art is the 1920s, where simple, rolling landscapes were sprinkled with distant, red-roofed houses and clumps of trees. I love Clarice Cliff's iconic ceramic surface designs and here I've translated her ideas into three dimensional form, so that you can create your own tiny world.

Difficulty - medium

You will need
For each hill (finished visible size approximately 8-12cm high outside of the egg cup)

- An average sized egg cup, about 5cm tall

- A good amount of green wool for the hill – at least 40cm, plus a little extra for layering

- Small amounts of white and red wool for the house, and a dark colour for the windows and door

- A small amount of light coloured wool if you are adding a winding path (just a few cm will do)

- Size 40 or size 42 felting needle (triangular or spiral)

- A felting mat

- Optional; dark thread for faux stitches, beads for the hill, fabric scraps for patches, needle and thread

GRETEL'S TIPS

- Adding darns and patches gives a sweet, careworn appearance, or leave the hill bare for a handy pin cushion

- This pattern can be adapted to fit any small receptacle - increase the amounts to make a tea cup landscape or add bundles of green round the cottage for a woodland effect.

1. Overstuff your egg cup with rolled up green wool. I've used a 40cm length, but judge what is the right amount for your particular cup. Needle the bottom part to firm it up.

2. You don't have to worry about the bottom being too tidy as it will be hidden by the egg cup, but check your progress until you think you've needled it enough to fill the egg cup.

3. Use the excess wool to shape a hill, pulling some of the top wool down, so that you make a gently tapering, rounded slope. Add more wool if needed.

4. Work the wool down, turning it frequently to keep it rounded. When it is firm and shaped nicely, add a thin layer of wool to neaten the surface (see page 12).

5. Use a small pinch of rolled up white wool and loosely shape your little house on your felting mat. Roll it up for a tower shape or work on four sides for a more traditional cottage.

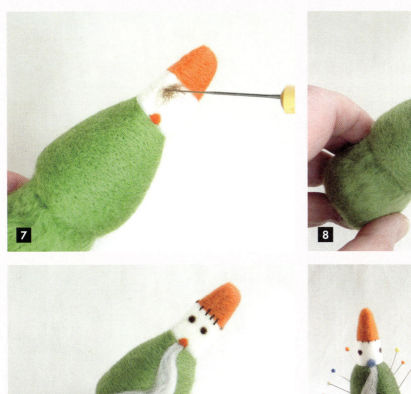

6. Needle the house onto the top of the hill and use another pinch of red or rust coloured wool to add a roof, using the tip of the needle to fine tune the edges.

7. Tiny windows and a door only need wisps of wool - it's surprising how just a few fibres will show up on white, so be sparing with the quantities you use.

8. Sew a few surface stitches to the cottage where the roof joins the walls. These add extra charm. They don't have to be perfect; in fact, they look nicer if they are a bit irregular.

9. To make a winding path, use a very skinny length of tapering wool and fix the tip in at the smallest point where the door is, spreading it out as it widens down the hill.

10. Leave the hill bare to use it as a pincushion, or add seed beads for a ditzy flower effect (see page 16). Stitch tiny darns (see page 14) and/or patches (see page 15).

49

ladybird, ladybird brooch

Whether you call them ladybirds or ladybugs, these cheerful little beetles are the very essence of hot, sunny summer days in the garden. With a bright scarlet colour scheme, this eye catching brooch will sit happily on a jacket or dress and keep you company on long summer days.

Difficulty - easy

You will need
For each ladybird (finished size approximately 4-5cm wide, 3cm in height)

■ Red or orange Merino wool, approx 20cm and a small amount of black wool

■ Size 40 or size 42 felting needle (triangular or spiral)

■ A felting mat

■ 2x large black seed beads or 3mm round onyx beads for the antenna

■ Strong black thread and a needle

■ A length of thick thread for the wing divide - I've used Perle here but you can also use standard DMC embroidery thread

GRETEL'S TIPS

■ Adapt the colours to make a yellow ladybird or use the same making technique to make different beetles.

■ Experiment with different embroidery stitches to make the spots. For instance, try using tiny seed stitches or French knots for a ditsy, scattered effect.

■ If brooches aren't your thing, leave off the pin back and sew a key holder to the ladybird's bottom to make a striking key ring holder.

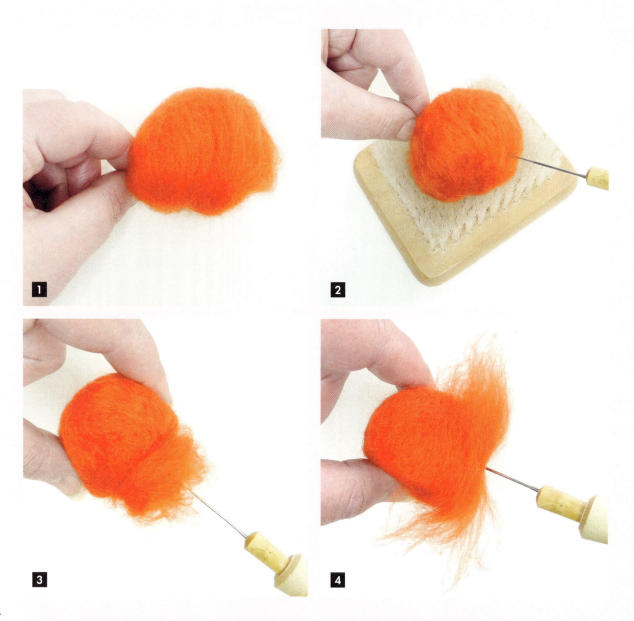

1. Take a length of wool measuring roughly 12-15cm long. Roll it up and pull the sides down, so that it forms a little hill.

2. Work on your mat to begin with, so that the underside remains flat. Shape a simple dome to create the shell of the ladybird. Add a little more wool on the top to add more height if required.

3. If the bottom is a bit sunken, just stuff some extra wool inside the empty space; this will bulk it out and allow you to create a really solid feel to your brooch.

4. Work the shell until it is firm, then cover it with a thin layer of wool (see page 12). Try to keep the surface neat so that the spots really pop out when you add them to the ladybird.

5. Use a small piece of black wool to cover a side section of the shell to make the head of the ladybird.

6. Divide the shell in half with a single long stitch of thick matching floss from top to bottom. Pull it snug to emphasis the divide between the wings.

7. Attach the brooch on the underside (see page 20).

8. Sew two beads onto the top of the head to create little eyes.

9. Finally, add the spots. Go completely dotty, by sewing on black beads (see page 16), needle felt them, or go for a bold statement with a couple of simple darns.

little lollipop trees

These adorable miniature toy town trees can be made to suit any season, but I've used light, summery colours here. Ragged Boro style stitching between the patches unifies the overall decoration and suggests tiny leaves. I've used vintage cotton reels, but if you don't have any, you can buy new blank ones from craft suppliers.

Difficulty - easy

You will need
For each tree (finished tree size approximately 10-12cm total height)

- Merino wool in light, summery colours and a small amount of brown
- Size 40 or size 42 felting needle (triangular or spiral)
- A felting mat
- An empty wooden cotton reel
- Embroidery thread – standard DMC six strand used here
- Sellotape
- 1x kebab stick
- Brown paper covered florists wire
- Needle and threads for stitching
- Scraps of material for patching
- Sharp pointed scissors, to make a hole in the tree

GRETEL'S TIPS

- This is a very adaptable pattern with scope for making all kinds of round and oval trees, so play around with your own shapes and sizes by altering the amount of wool used.
- Embellish your tree with contrasting seed beads for a striking polka dot effect.
- If you don't have paper covered wire, use wool or a thicker DMC embroidery thread to wrap the tree trunk in.

1. Start with two pieces of wool, one small bundle for the core and a longer piece, roughly 15x4cm in length. Place the core in the middle of the outer strip over the core to completely enclose it.

2. Needle it into a tapering, bulbous shape, adding as many extra layers as needed until it firms up and is the size you want. This should be in proportion to your cotton reel, so that it looks nicely balanced.

3. Add little patches (see page 15). I've used pieces of vintage fabric attached using very simple stitches with running stitches in between, and thin cotton.

4. Use a scrap of Sellotape to fix one end of the embroidery thread to the reel, winding it tightly around the spool so it's completely covered. Tuck the other end of the thread neatly under the wound thread.

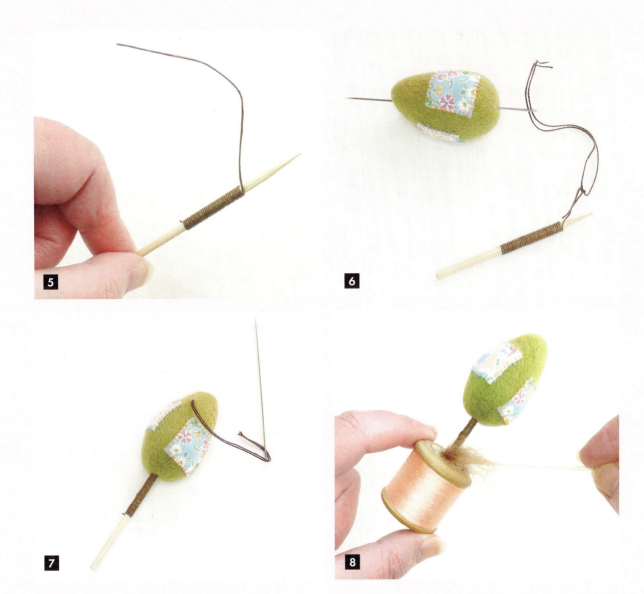

5. Cut off a short length from the pointed end of the kebab stick and wind the wire neatly around it in a single layer, finishing off just below the tip. Make a small loop on one end.

6. Tie a piece of thread around the wire loop. Using pointed scissors, make a deep indent in the bottom of the tree, thread a needle and pull the kebab point up and into the body of the tree.

7. Pull the point of the kebab stick so it is snug inside the tree and there is no bare wood showing. Bring the needle out away from the tip and pulling the thread free, snip the ends off.

8. Stuff half of the centre of the reel with brown wool and place the end of the kebab stick inside. Then fill in around the trunk bottom until it is holding the tree firmly upright, without any wobble.

ring 'o' roses wrist wrap

Charmingly stylish with Art Deco overtones, this chunky wrist wrap is a bold summer accessory which can be made to colour match any outfit. You can either stitch the roses to a wide ribbon or tape of your choice, or sew onto a simple bracelet fastener.

Difficulty - easy

You will need
A selection of Merino wools in the colours of your chosen roses; small amounts per flower

■ Size 40 or size 42 felting needle (triangular or spiral)

■ A felting mat

■ Needle and threads that match the colour of the roses and the ribbon (if using)

■ To fasten – a generous length of ribbon - I've used 40mm burgundy organza here, or

■ A bracelet fastening - I've used a 10mm rose gold lobster claw with a 10mm rose gold jump ring

GRETEL'S TIPS

■ This pattern can be adapted for different uses; turn a large rose into a brooch by fixing a pin to the back (see page 20) or make a pretty, trailing length of Midsummer bunting by using different sized blooms sewn onto green ribbon or cord.

■ Have fun experimenting with different colour palettes to match your outfits.

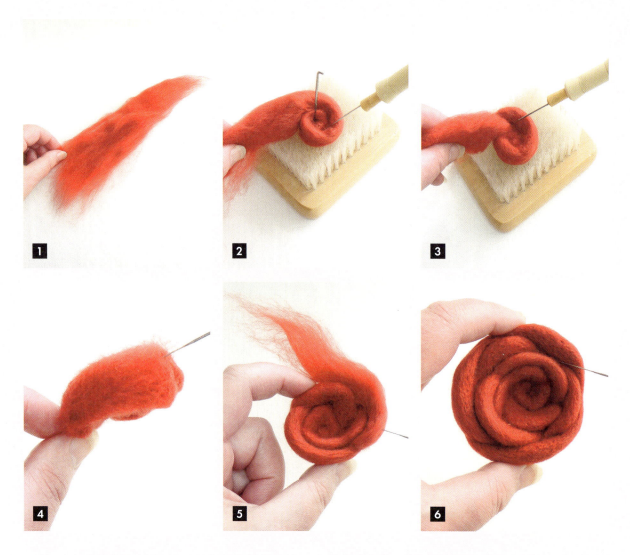

1. Take a length of wool, remove some of the width and spread it out slightly so that you have a tapering length. I've used about 20cm here to start off with.

2. Anchor the tip of the wool onto the mat using a spare needle, wind a little wool around it and needle into place, before snugly winding more around it to create the tight centre of the rose.

3. Once the wool is fixed, remove the spare needle. Continue to wind the wool around in a spiral, keeping the shape round. From time to time, twist the wool, to make a break in the petals.

4. When you get to the end of the length of wool, remove the rose from the mat. Work the last loose fibres down, blending them into the body of the wool.

5. If you want a bigger flower, needle another strip of wool onto the outer side and continue to work as before, building up the height of the rose with larger pieces of wool until you are finished.

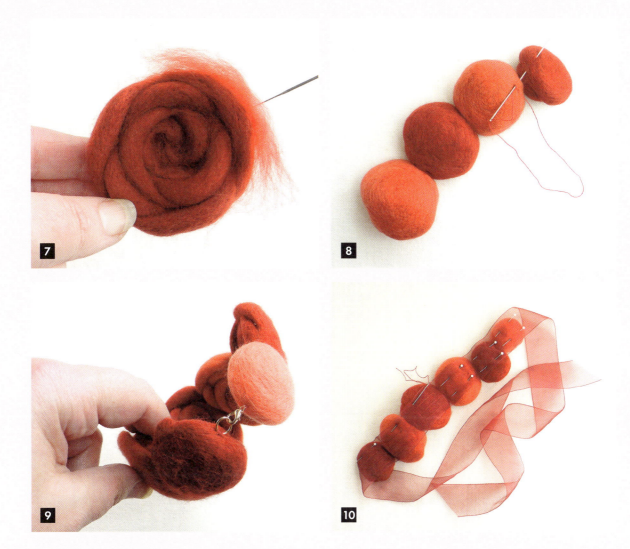

6. With the needle at a slight slant, dig the tip between the petals, using a gentle, sideways chiselling motion to emphasise the breaks between them.

7. Once you are happy with the size, use tiny pieces of wool to layer over the underside and outer petals of the rose to smooth the surface (see page 12).

8. Make enough roses in a variety of colours and sizes until you have enough to cover your wrist. Stitch the undersides firmly together in your chosen order, starting from the central flower and working outwards.

9. If you are using a bracelet fastening, stitch each component to the underside of the outermost roses, using a strong, matching thread.

10. If you are using ribbon or tape, pin the roses to it before stitching them on securely using a few long stitches per flower. Finally cut the ribbon ends to size, leaving plenty for a nice looking bow.

so sweet strawberries

So simple, so sweet, these little strawberries make a delightful table decoration, a thoughtful Midsummer gift or even a bijou pincushion. I've used a basic stump-work technique to give the leaves a sumptuous finish. Strawberries aren't always red, so try using off-whites and rich pinks to add variety to your arrangement.

Difficulty - easy

You will need
For each strawberry (finished size approximately 5-6cm in length)

- A small amount of Merino wool in the colours of your choice (reds, off-whites, deep pinks) and scraps of green for the leaves

- Size 40 or size 42 felting needle (triangular or spiral)

- A felting mat

- Needle and thick embroidery floss such as standard DMC or Perle

- Seed beads and/or thread for embellishment

- Optional 6mm glass pearl bead or similar for a top stump

GRETEL'S TIPS

- Make sure your strawberry is firmly felted before decorating, so the beads or stitches don't sink into the wool. If it is very 'fuzzy', trim any stray fibres with small, sharp scissors, so they won't get tangled in your embellishments.

- Try making little felted wire leaves to add to your strawberries, using the basic techniques in the 'Tumbling Autumn Leaves' pattern (see page 76).

1. Take a good pinch of roving, and roll it up with the fibres lying vertically down the body. Arrange the wool so that there is more at one end than the other and start needling into a strawberry shape.

2. Add extra wool to enlarge the strawberry to the size you require. Keep the fibres laying in the same direction lengthways, to get a neater finish. Work until shaped and firm.

3. Use little scraps of green wool to add plump leaves to the top. If you are going to sew over these, they should be very sturdy, so they will support the overlaying stitches.

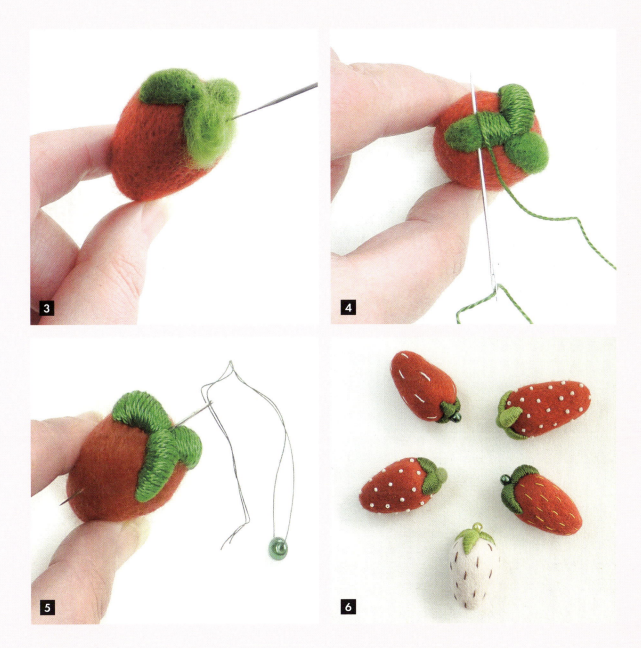

4. Using a thick embroidery floss, cover the leaves with a closely sewn satin stitch. Keep the tension even without pulling too tightly, while keeping the stitches snug to the leaf.

5. Top your strawberry off with a needle felted stump or stitch on a matching bead. You can also use the

bead hole to turn your strawberry into a little dangle with a piece of thread.

6. Seed beads (see page 16) and scattered straight stitches (see page 16) can be used to emulate the dimples on the fruit, or leave plain if you are using it as a bijou pin cushion.

chapter three: autumn

When the season changes and the evenings draw in, it's time to cosy up by the fire with tea, cake and a pile of warm felting wools. Create a woodland wonderland of embellished acorns and decorated toadstools, with a scattering of colourful autumnal leaves or brighten a favourite jumper with a sweet, nestling squirrel brooch with a delightfully sly slinky fox bangle peeking out from under the sleeve.

adorable acorns

Is there anything more autumnal than an acorn? For this project, I love to use warm, earthy colours that allow contrasting beads and stitches to pop out. They are so quick to make that you can easily create a colourful set for a seasonal tree display or make larger ones for a bowl display in an afternoon.

Difficulty - easy

You will need
For each medium sized acorn (finished size approximately 7-8cm in length)

- Merino wools, in the colours of your choice - approx 25cm for the nut and 20cm for the cap, plus covering wool

- Size 40 or size 42 felting needle (triangular or spiral)

- A felting mat

- Optional - seed beads of various sizes, mixed threads for darning and stitching, small jump rings for dangles, fabric scraps for patches

GRETEL'S TIPS

- Add a brooch back to a small acorn (see page 20) and you have the sweetest little jacket accessory for chilly October days.

- To make smaller or larger acorns, simply halve or double the amount of wool used and follow the pattern as shown. If you want to make a same sized set of acorns, measure the length of wools first for the nuts and the caps so that you can duplicate them easily.

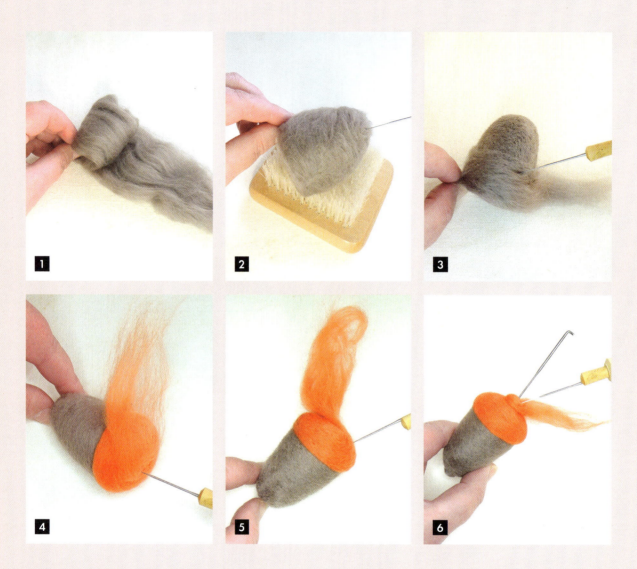

1. Use a slender length of wool - here I have used approximately 25x3cm - and widen it out a little. Roll it up so that you have a squidgy bundle, with more at one end where the base will be.

2. Start needling, turning as you work. The bottom of the nut should be flat and straight and the top gently rounded, so that it resembles a mini bee hive.

3. When it's feeling quite firm, add a little extra wool to the bottom, to widen it out where it will meet the cap and fill out the nut with more wool until the shape is just right.

4. Take another smaller length of wool measuring approximately 20x2cm. Fix one end to the base of the nut and begin needling it around the circumference and onto the base.

5. Continue winding the wool and needling it into a small hat shaped dome. If you run out of wool, you can add small amounts, building up the cap until

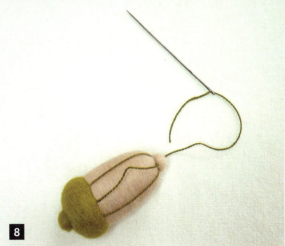

you're happy with the shape.

6. Add a small nubble to each end, using wisps of wool. You can use a spare needle as a temporary centre point, using the tip of your working felting needle to twizzle it around.

7. Finish off by adding thin layers of wool to neaten the surface (see page 12) and work it until it is firm enough to decorate.

8. Make pin stripes from long lengths of embroidery floss run from the under edge of the cup to the top of the acorn. Different thread thicknesses vary the effect.

9. Beautify your acorn with seed beads (see page 16) tiny darns (see page 14), patches (see page 15) and decorative embroidery.

10. Add a loop of thread to turn it into an autumnal dangle. (See page 21). I've used a dark, chocolate brown Perle thread on all of my acorns, for uniformity.

sleepy squirrel brooch

This brooch is made from one length of wool; only the tiny ears are added later, so take this into account when you are starting the tail, making sure you leave enough for the body and the head. This sleepy squirrel will add a charming autumn touch to your jackets and coats as the weather gets colder.

Difficulty - medium

You will need
For each brooch (finished size approx 6cm tall)

- Merino roving in a rich red, about 35cm in total, small amount of white for the tummy and optional black or brown for the nose

- Size 40 or size 42 felting needle (triangular or spiral)

- A felting mat

- 25mm brooch back

- Black seed bead

- Optional thick black thread if sewing the nose

- Optional threads for darns and stitches

GRETEL'S TIPS

- Take care when positioning the brooch back, so that your squirrel isn't top heavy when attached to your clothing.
  - I use round headed pins to temporarily fix the pin, so that I can judge how it will balance before sewing it on permanently.

- Add a tiny textile patch to the tail instead of a darn, for extra cuteness.

- If you want a wide awake squirrel, use a round bead instead of a seed bead for the eye, such as a 2 or 3mm black onyx bead.

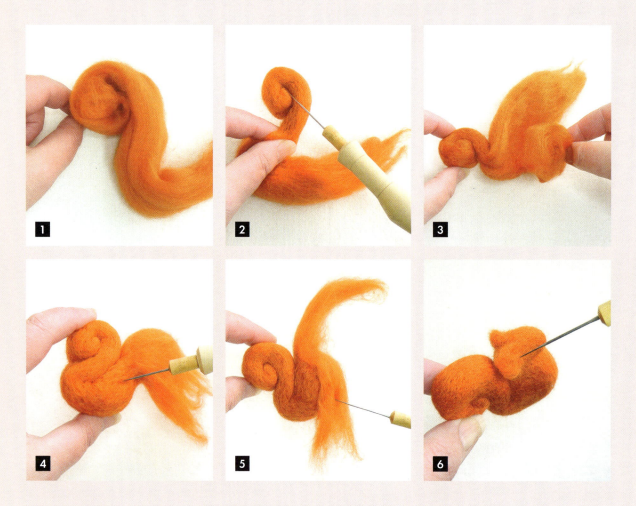

1. Take a length of wool approx 30x4cm. Roll one end up to make a fat spiral with a little over for the remainder of the tail. Pull the edges of the roving round and begin needling.

2. Use the side of the needle to chisel a little curlicue into the end of the tail. Work the tail until it is shaped; it should have some 'squidge', so that it can be easily joined to the body.

3. Spread the wool out from the base of the tail and insert an extra plug of wool inside the loose tummy area to fill it out, enclosing it before working the main part of the body.

4. Hold the tail against the body as you work, needling them together to keep them in place. They should be joined so that the tail sits against the rounded back.

5. Once you have a nicely plump body, split the remaining wool into two. Reserve a small amount of leftover wool for the head and pull the extra wool down to add to the tummy.

6. The nut shaped head should be tilting downwards and joined to the chest, as if the squirrel is dozing off. Use two tiny scraps of wool to add a pair of ears.

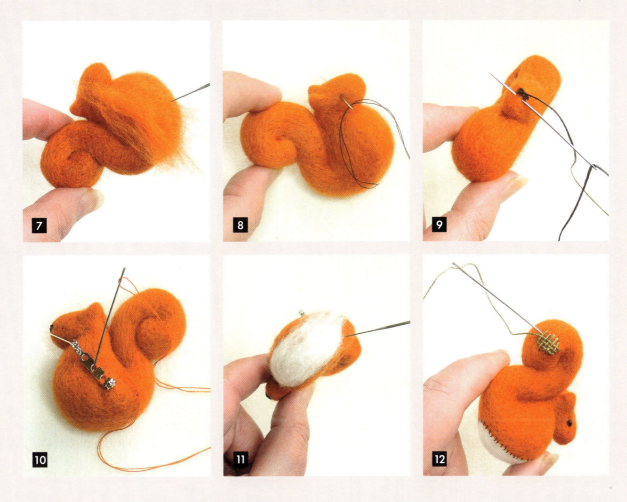

7. When you're happy with the overall look of things, add a fine layer of wool (see page 12) to bring the whole design together, working until everything is sturdy.

8. Snip a little slit into the eye area and sew in a threaded black seed bead. It should be inserted on its side, so that your squirrel has a half lidded, dozing appearance.

9. Use a few dark fibres to needle felt a tiny triangular nose onto the face, or sew one using a thick black thread. Three stitches should be enough, in descending size, like a teddy bear nose.

10. Sew on the brooch back and overlay with extra wool for security (see page 20). I've placed mine in a horizontal position, so that it will balance well when worn.

11. Layer the tummy with an oval of white wool, using the tip of your needle to get a clean divide between the colours before adding simple stitches around the edge in a contrasting thread.

12. For a final touch, darn a sweet little patch onto the tail - I've used Perle embroidery thread, for a bit of extra sheen.

tumbling autumn leaves

This free range pattern uses what is called a flat felting technique. This means you keep the roving on the mat as you work, needling directly down into it, before peeling it off to use it like a piece of fabric. You may want to use two or three needles in a multi-holder to speed up the process.

Difficulty - easy

You will need

- Autumn coloured wools of your choice, small amounts for each leaf dependent on size

- Size 40 or size 42 felting needle (triangular or spiral)

- A felting mat

- Lengths of brown paper covered florists wire or whatever bendable wire you have

- Needle and embroidery floss of good thickness, such as Perle or standard six strand DMC

GRETEL'S TIPS

- Be creative and bold with your colours and 'paint' with the wools as you're blend them together.

- The wire stems are twisted untidily on purpose, so that when they are wrapped, they form a naturally knobbly twig effect. I've shaped my leaves freehand, but you can draw them out first to use as a guide. Alternatively, you can find leaf outlines by image searching 'leaf shape' online. Make a variety of sizes for maximum impact.

1. Make a loop at one end of the wire, twisting it round and down to make the stalk and leaf shape. Any spare wire can either be wound back up the stalk or snipped off.

2. The amount of wool you need should be approximately twice the size of your wire shape.

3. Mix your wools together, fluffing them up to mix the fibres together like candy floss. I've used two main colours, with a small amount of a third colour for highlights.

4. Once you're happy with the blend, pull the fibres into short lengths, so that they lie horizontally the same way and then lay them flat on the felting mat.

5. Needle downwards and evenly, turning the wool over from time to time to prevent it sticking to the mat, until it feels like a piece of fabric.

6. Place the leaf shape onto the wool (you may want to remove any large amounts of excess material) and fold the edges over the wire, needling them into place.

7. Work the wool down on both sides until it is fairly flat and fits closely around the wire edge so that you

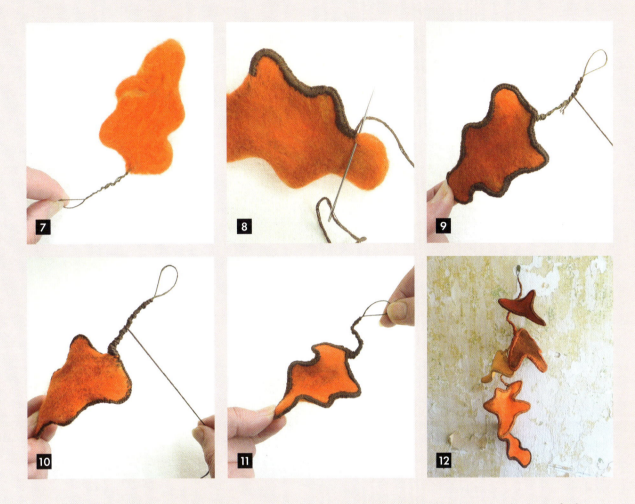

can comfortably sew the felt onto it.

8. Use a tightly packed blanket stitch to edge around the sides, until the outline is bound all around. There's no need to knot the thread, as any ends can vanish into the felt.

9. Once the leaf edge is bound, tie an end of thread around the top of the stalk, leaving the loop bare. Wind around and down the stem, hiding the thread end under the first wraps.

10. You don't have to be to perfect with your wrapping - extra padding around lumpy bits and

breaks in the thread give a natural, twiggy feel.

11. Tidy up the felt surface on both sides with tiny, shallow jabs, before bending the leaf into its final position. Use the inner wire to curl the ends, giving it a wind blown appearance.

12. By looping the stalks over each other, you can make little dangling bunches and garlands. Alternatively, they can be hung singly from dark threads or scattered as a table dressing.

slinky fox bangles

There is a Celtic feel to this slinky fox bangle design, making for a striking statement piece that will go well with warmer autumn clothing and cosy woollen jumpers. Use the wispy ends of the wool to your advantage as they will naturally form the tapering tail and pointy muzzle of your fox.

Difficulty - medium

You will need
For each bangle (finished size - variable)

- Merino wool in rusty brown - length is dependent on wrist size, but 40-50cm should be enough for a small to average wrist. Scrap of white wool for the tail tip

- Size 40 or size 42 felting needle (triangular or spiral)

- A felting mat

- 2x black seed beads or 2mm onyx beads

- Strong black thread and a needle

- Optional hook and eye - size 0 used here

GRETEL'S TIPS

- The bangle is made from one length of wool divided into the long body, the tail and the head, which can be joined with a hidden hook and eye to fasten it with. You will need to use your judgment for wool length, as everyone has a different sized wrist, so I haven't included measurements, but you can easily adjust the position of the hook and eye so that the bangle fits and feels comfortable.

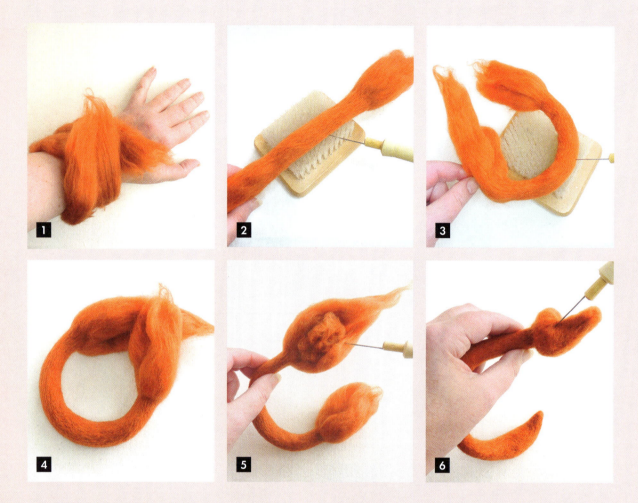

1. Wrap the roving around your wrist so that you can gauge how much you will need. Leave roughly 10-12cm extra for the tail and 6-8cm for the head, which can be added to or reduced.

2. Start needling from the centre of the wool and work outwards, shaping a long, even, round strip. If it is too thin for your liking, add a bit of extra roving on top, lengthwise.

3. When the wool starts to firm up, gently bend it into a curve and carry on working; it doesn't have to be a full circle, just enough to cover about three quarters of your wrist.

4. Check the length around your wrist until you have a shaped bangle to fit around your wrist with a bit of excess overlap on top; the long tail and head will cover the rest.

5. Using the longest tuft of wool at one end, shape the tail into a tapering curve. Plump it out by stuffing a plug of wool inside the middle before working it until it is firm.

6. Form the head by pushing the wool inwards; the end wool becomes the pointy muzzle and the denser part is shaped into a chiselled face with an angular brow where the eyes will go.

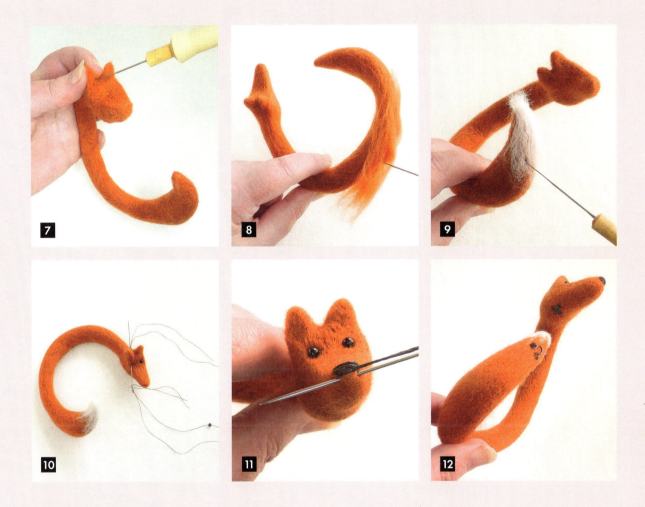

7. Use two equal sized scraps of wool for the triangular ears and needle them directly onto the head, using your fingers to hold the wool into points as you work.

8. At this stage you should make final alterations, adding more bulk to the body or tail if needed, to thicken them up, before covering everything with a fine layer of wool (see page 12).

9. Tip the tail with scant white fibres, using the tip of the needle to drag the wispy ends down onto the main tail so that they gently blend in.

10. Sew in the eyes, using the front facing method (see page 18), using small, round beads - I've used 3mm black onyx ones, but good sized seed beads will also work.

11. Stitch a tiny nose with thick black thread, sewing three or four diminishing stitches horizontally, like a teddy bear nose.

12. Finally, sew on the hook and eye after judging where each element should go for the bangle to fit comfortably, putting the hook underneath the chin and placing the eye near the end of the tail.

enchanted woodland toadstools

I still remember seeing my first toadstool at the age of six years old. It was a large Fly Agaric growing under a tree in a wood; the typical red and white spotted 'fairy toadstool'. I was fascinated by its bright colour and otherworldliness. Since then I've had a lifelong love of fungi and they are my favourite things to make.

Difficulty - medium

You will need
For each medium sized toadstool (finished size approximately 6-8cm tall).

- 30-35cm cap wool of your choice and 25-30 pale stalk wool

- Some wisps of green or brown wool for a grass or earth effect.

- Size 40 or size 42 felting needle (triangular or spiral)

- A felting mat

- Optional threads, seed beads and fabric scraps for decoration

GRETEL'S TIPS

- This is a lovely free range pattern, where you can make your toadstools as oddly shaped and contorted as you like. Try lengthening the stalk by increasing the measurements and play around with different colour combinations. There are so many ways to decorate a toadstool, but sometimes it's nice to leave them plain and natural, depending on the look you are going for.

- Look up toadstools online to get inspiration; you'll be amazed at the variety of shapes and colours.

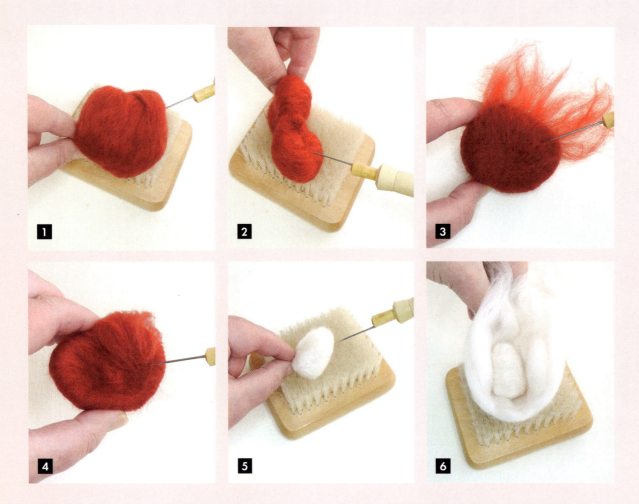

1. Take a small amount of wool in the cap colour of your choice - roughly 20-25cm will do. Fold it over to make a small bundle and begin needling it into a round shape.

2. When the wool firms up, create a contorted shape by bending the cap as you work, until it holds its position, adding a little more wool here and there, to make extra lumps and bumps.

3. When the cap is quite firm and you're happy with the shape, cover it with thin patches of wool (see page 12) to create a smooth surface. Use short tufts, working around the cap.

4. Tuck any extra end fibres under the cap and needle them down. Don't worry too much about neatness, as this part will be covered by the gills later.

5. The stalk is made separately, before joining it to the cap. Take a good pinch of wool, fold it over and shape a little egg, to fill the bottom of the stalk.

6. Using a length of wool measuring roughly 25cm, place the filling in the middle (fat end down) and bring the sides up and around, to enclose it, closing off any side gaps.

7. Form a bulbous bottom and work some of the main

stem into shape, leaving a portion of the end fibres free (these form the gills later on).

8. When the stalk is formed, spread the remaining loose fibres out evenly into a circle, so they look like an open flower.

9. Place the stalk onto the underside of the cap, needling the loose fibres onto the underside. Try to keep the fibres straight so that they resemble the fine gills of a real toadstool.

10. If you have any loose end fibres sticking out, fold them back and down into the stalk, creating a neat

edge between the gills and the cap.

11. Add some scant fibres of grass green or earthy brown to the base of the stalk, dragging them up the stem for a wispy finish. Try combining colours for a natural effect.

12. Decorate with tiny darns (see page 14), patches (see page 15) and simple stitching (see page 13), using matching embroidery floss to make a magical woodland dangle (see page 21).

chapter four: winter

Winter is when needle felting comes into its own. These easy projects are designed to bring beauty and joy to your celebrations. Spun cotton pears and little Arctic geese will give a vintage atmosphere to your holiday décor, while playfully coloured advent bells add bright colour accents. Nestle a charming gingerbread village at the bottom of your tree and finish it off with a hare tree topper.

winter geese

One of the first signs of winter approaching is when I hear flocks of geese flying over my cottage, practising for their long migration. If I am quick, I can dash outside to see their impressive V formation as they pass over, their haunting cries disappearing into the dusk.

Difficulty - easy

You will need
For each small goose (finished size approximately 10cm in length)

- Merino wool, in white, grey or brown, about 25cm split lengthwise to give you a width of 4cm

- Size 40 or size 42 felting needle (triangular or spiral)

- A felting mat

- 1x gold inked cocktail stick beak (see page 19) or you can simply needle felt one.

- 2x black seed beads or 2mm onyx beads

- Strong black thread and a needle

- Thin single strand embroidery cotton for darns and stitches (Danish Flower thread used here)

- Embroidery thread or thin yarn for the dangle

- A small jump ring (8mm bronze ring used here)

GRETEL'S TIPS

- This is a simple pattern that can be upscaled to any size you want, but these measurements will give quick results, so that you can make several for a magical, ephemeral display. Use soft whites and warm browns or greys to echo natural feather colours, with tiny understated darns here and there for an age-worn appearance.

1. Start with a small length of wool measuring roughly 12x4cm. Fold it in half so that it forms a long droplet shape, tuck in any loose fibres and needle the wool until it begins to firm up.

2. Take a longer length of wool, about 16x4cm. Fold it lengthwise around the core you've just made and needle it down to join the two together.

3. Continue working and shaping, flattening the back and adding a little more wool to the tummy and sides to plump the body out, if needed.

4. Add two wings, using two equal sized scraps of wool. These can be fixed straight onto the body and tweaked into shape with the tip of the needle.

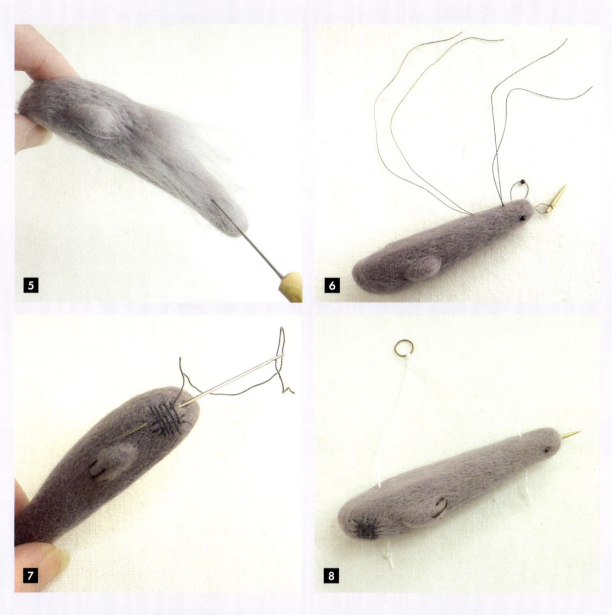

5. Cover the whole body with a fine layer of wool (see page 12). Round the head off, making sure it is firm enough to fix the beak in.

6. Put in the cocktail stick beak (see page 19) then sew in the two tiny eyes, using the sideways method (see page 18).

7. One or two miniature darns (see page 14) can be sewn onto the body, using thick cotton or Danish Flower thread. I've also added three simple stitches to each wing, for a rustic effect.

8. Loop the thread onto a jump ring. Using a needle, take one thread end into the tail and the other into the neck. Tie a knot in each end and pull into the body.

spun cotton style pears

These folksy little fruits emulate antique spun cotton decorations, popular in Victorian times. I have used a warm, light beige wool as a base, to suggest an aged feel. The top colours are finely dragged with the needle tip, to resemble painted cotton fibres and little paper wired leaves authenticate the vintage theme.

Difficulty - easy

You will need

For each small pear (finished size approximately 5cm in length)

- Merino wool; about 20cm base wool of warm off-white or light fawn, main colours of greens and yellows, fragments of warm reds, pinks, oranges and brown for accents

- Size 40 or size 42 felting needle (triangular or spiral)

- A felting mat

- Small mulberry paper wired rose leaves, 12mm used here

- Needle and thread

- Optional - transparent glass seed beads – Miyuki crystal, size 15/0 used here, beading needle, invisible thread

GRETEL'S TIPS

- Alter the size by adjusting the amount of wool you use. Play around with warm colour combinations and add tiny glass beads for a sparkling faux glitter finish.

- Use just one colour for a more striking effect and add a contrasting darn or two to your pear.

- Instead of using paper leaves, make felted ones, using the 'Tumbling Autumn Leaves' pattern (see page 76).

95

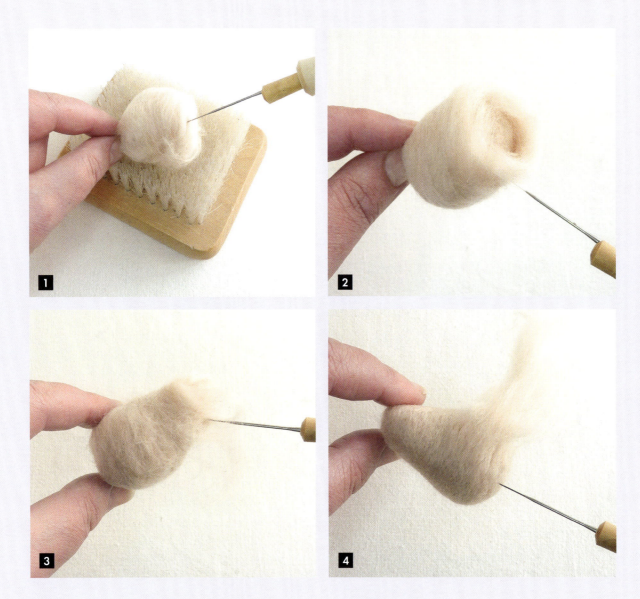

1. Roll up a good pinch of base wool, about 15x4 cm and shape it into a core for the pear bottom. It should be the size of a large grape and still quite soft before you move on to the next step.

2. Wrap a slender length of wool around the core and needle it down. Some of the wool should be fixed to the underneath of the pear whilst leaving the upper fibres loose.

3. Wind another small length of wool to make the top of the pear, joining it onto the main body. Needle it down until it is the same consistency as the rest of the body.

4. Now you have a complete fruit, build the layers of base wool up until it is pleasantly plump and quite firm in texture, ready for the final colours.

5. Apply the main colour, covering most of the pear, but leaving the odd gap here and there, to expose the base, so that it resembles the painted fibres of a spun cotton ornament.

6. Add wispy slivers of wool in warm tones, dragging them over and around the surface to create a painterly effect. Use the tip of the needle to blend them together.

7. Loop the leaf wire and make a hole in the top of the pear. Tie a piece of thread onto the wire and pull the excess wire into the felt with a needle, so that only the loop and leaf show.

8. For extra frosty sparkle, stitch tiny glass seed beads (see page 16) to the surface, using a beading needle and invisible thread, or thin cotton thread that matches the tone of your pear.

advent bells

These jolly little advent bells are inspired by a set of German hand painted wooden decorations that I bought many years ago at a Christmas market when I was seventeen. I fell in love with their simple cheerfulness and have treasured them ever since. They will look wonderful on any style Christmas tree.

Difficulty - easy

You will need
For each bell (finished size approximately 10cm in length)

- Small amounts of Merino wools in your chosen colours
- Size 40 or size 42 felting needle (triangular or spiral)
- A felting mat
- Seed beads and embroidery threads for decoration
- Thread for hanging

GRETEL'S TIPS

- My interpretation of these advent bells uses a vintage inspired palette for a bright mid-century look, but they can be made in any other colours to suit your own holiday décor. As with the other patterns, you can scale them up to create bigger bells, although this version is a quick and easy way to create a gorgeous coordinated collection.

1. Take two equal short pieces of wool each measuring no more than 12cm in length. Split one of the pieces into two, lengthwise, to reduce the width, giving you three pieces of wool.

2. Place one of the smaller pieces of wool onto the lower half of the larger piece and roll it up; the fatter end of the roll will be the wide bottom of your bell.

3. Needle the wool into a simple bell shape. Turn it regularly as you work, to ensure a good roundness and consistent overall texture, but keep the bottom flat.

4. When the wool is firm and you are happy with the shape, add a thin layer of wool (see page 12) to neaten the surface, using some of the wool you put aside earlier.

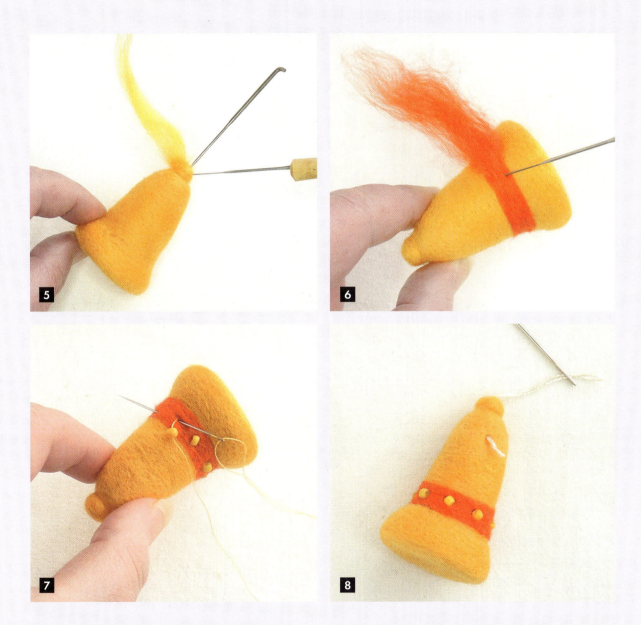

5. Take a spare needle and stick it into the top of the bell. Wind a long wisp of wool around it, needling it into a round nubble. When it is firm and shaped, remove the spare needle.

6. You can leave your bell as one plain colour, or add a band or two of a complementary colour; Play around with different colour contrasts.

7. Decorate the bells with simple embroidery - cross stitches around the bands and bright seed beads are easy ways to add eye catching patterns.

8. Use a loop of embroidery floss pulled into the top (see page 21) to make it into a vibrant hanging bauble. I've used a neutral off-white on all of my bells, to unify the collection.

marvellous mr hare tree topper

This stylised, slender running hare resembles a cut out piece of folk art, making him a stand out decoration when he is attached to the tree top, rather like a weather vane. Mr Hare is a larger project which will take a few hours, so it's perfect for a quiet, cosy winter's day, with hot tea and a mince pie to keep you going.

Difficulty - medium/hard

You will need
For one hare (finished size approximately 20cm in length from toe to toe)

- Merino wools in light fawn about 80cm, small amounts of darker brown, small amounts of white

- Size 40 or size 42 felting needle (triangular or spiral)

- A felting mat

- 2x round black beads - 3mm onyx bead used here

- Strong black thread and a needle

- Thicker black thread for a stitched nose (or you can needle felt one)

- Red embroidery floss or Danish Flower thread for a small decorative darn

- 1 metre of wide ribbon or tape - I've used 40mm wired red Hessian tape, so that the bow will hold its shape when tied to the top of the tree

1. Take a length of roving measuring 35cm and another measuring 25cm. Place the smaller length onto the centre of the larger one. The middle part will form the body of the hare.
2. Work the central area of the wool to shape the trunk of the hare, leaving equal amounts of loose fibre either side. This will make the legs, head and ears later.

3. While the wool is still soft, open up the tummy area on the left hand side and insert a good plug of muddled up roving. Enclose the outer wool around it and carry on working.
4. As you work, hold the body in a gentle sinuous curve; the fatter end should be higher than the front so that your hare will appear to be running.

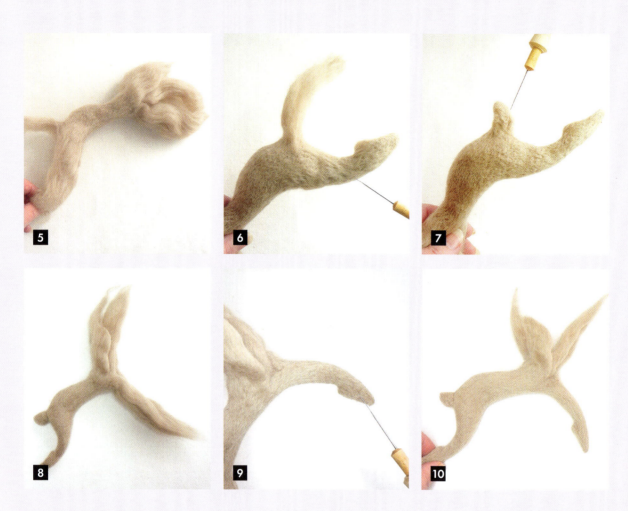

5. Once the trunk is firm and shaped, divide the wool on the left hand side into two - a small piece at the top for the tail and the larger piece to make an outstretched back leg.

6. Shape the back leg, arranging the wool so that there is a good amount for the chunky thigh and foot. You may need to add extra wool to get it well proportioned.

7. Shape the small piece into a tail by tucking any loose end fibres over into a little roll. It should be fatter where it joins the body end and stick out with a slightly curved shape.

8. Divide the wool on the right side into two – about two thirds for the ears and head and a third for the front legs.

9. The length of the outstretched front leg should be in proportion to the back, so remove any excess wool and use it to bulk up the top of the leg, before shaping the rest of it.

10. Divide the final loose wool into two, a larger part for the ears and a smaller part for the head. If you don't have enough, then add some extra wool where needed.

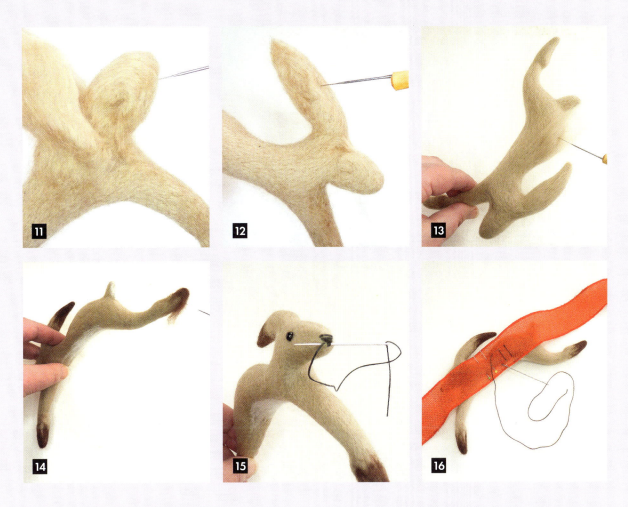

11. Roll the smaller piece of wool up to make a nut shape and form the long, outstretched head, joining it to the body and smoothing out any folds and gaps.

12. Shape the long ears in one piece, as you did the legs, joining the base to the top of the head and using your fingers to pinch the wool together at the tip, to get a good point.

13. Now that you have a complete hare you can add extra wool to any areas you think may need it, before covering it with a thin layer of wool to neaten the surface (see page 12).

14. Use scant amounts of wool to add white points to the tummy and tail area and dark points to the ear and foot tips, before sewing a little darn onto his rump.

15. Sew in the eyes, using the sideways method (see page 18) and add a triangular nose, which can be made up of a few stitches using thick black thread or needle felted using a dark wool.

16. Fix your hare to the middle of the ribbon with a few good stitches so that he doesn't wobble, then tie him to the tree with a generous bow before cutting the ribbon ends down to size.

gingerbread wonderland

This fairytale village is designed to be a miniature under-tree decoration, but you can also turn each piece into a hanging decoration by adding some thread loops. Create a collection of different sized houses and trees; make them larger or smaller by adjusting the amounts of wool used and follow the same process.

Difficulty - easy

You will need
For trees and house (sizes variable)

- Merino wools in warm gingerbread tones and white for snow. Small amounts needed for each item

- A felting mat

- Size 40 or size 42 felting needle (triangular or spiral)

- Extra decorations: various thicknesses of white threads and flosses (single and double stranded), white seed beads (opaque white Toho, size 11/0 used here)

GRETEL'S TIPS

- I've suggested some basic snow effects, but there are all kinds of possibilities for decoration, including appliqué and embroidery, adding buttons, ric rac trim and lace, to make your village unique to you.

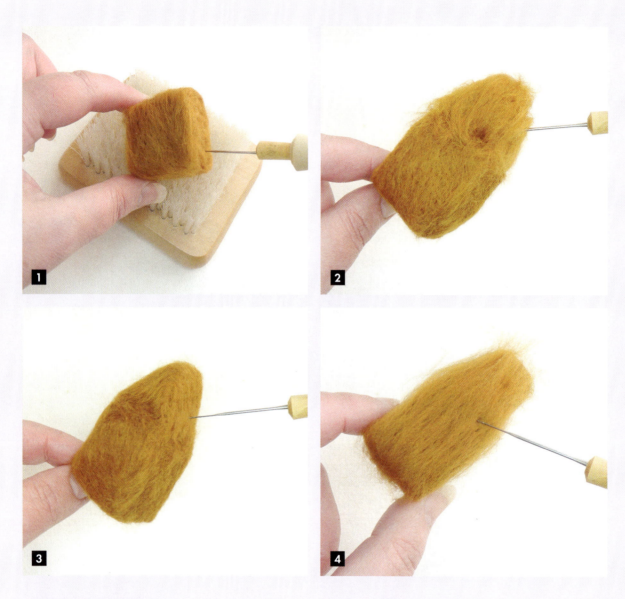

GINGERBREAD HOUSE

1. Take a small amount of wool - I've used roughly 20cm here - and roll it up into a bundle. Begin needling the house base, working on all six sides to make a square or oblong.

2. When it is shaped and still soft, add another piece of wool to the top and join the two together, forming the roof as you do so, until it is one whole unit.

3. You may want to add extra bits of wool here and there, until you have the size and shape you are aiming for. Then work the wool until it is shaped and firm.

4. Add a fine layer of wool (see page 12) to the house and neaten off the surface, so that it is ready for the extra snowy decorations.

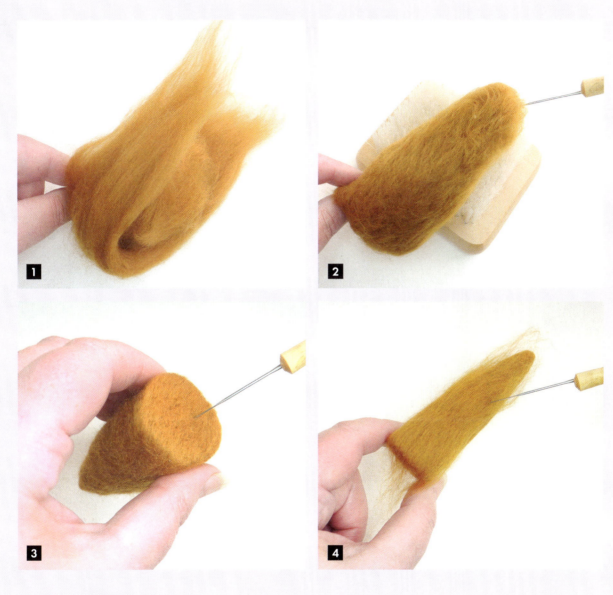

GINGERBREAD TREE

1. Take a length of wool - I've used about 25cm here - and spread it out. Make a filling core from a pinch of wool, place it in the middle of the length and fold it over, halving the length.

2. Shape a cone, turning as you work to keep the roundness. Tuck any loose top fibres over and back into the top.

3. Make sure the bottom is flat, so that your tree will stand up. Use your fingers to hold the wool in place as you work, to get a good, circular edge.

4. When the wool is firm and shaped, cover the tree with a fine layer of wool (see page 12) and work it down until it is smooth and ready to embellish.

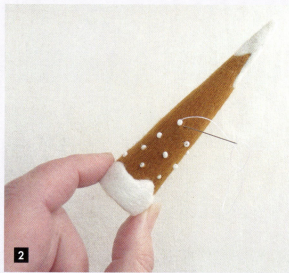

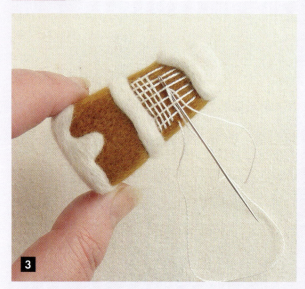

ADDING SNOW EFFECTS

1. Use white wool to shape natural snowfall, using the tip of your needle to make a rippled edge. Add extra wool to make tiny dribbles of snow, to look like dripping icing.

2. Stitch white seed beads to the surfaces to emulate falling snowflakes, in a scattered pattern (see page 16).

3. Doors, windows and folksy hearts can be needle felted with tiny amounts of white wool. Use loose weave darns (see page 14) to make trellis roof patterns and window panes.

4. Add piped icing decorations with long and cross stitches. Use a variety of thread thicknesses, taking each end slightly under the edges to blend them in.

wool suppliers

Merino wool is widely available to buy online, but my favourite companies for wools and other needle felting accessories are:

UK
Wingham Wool Work Ltd
70 Main Street
Wentworth
Rotherham
South Yorkshire
S62 7TN
www.winghamwoolwork.co.uk

Adelaide Walker
Unit 22, Town Head Mills
Main Street
Addingham
Ilkley
West Yorkshire
LS29 0PD
www.adelaidewalker.co.uk

World of Wool
Unit 8, The Old Railway Goods Yard
Scar Lane
Milnsbridge
Huddersfield
West Yorkshire
HD3 4PE
www.worldofwool.co.uk

USA
Living Felt
2440 E Highway 290
Ste E1
Dripping Springs
TX 78620
www.feltingsupplies.livingfelt.com

USA
The Woolery
859 E Main St
Frankfort
KY 40601
www.woolery.com

The Felted Ewe
1261 Parkside Dr
Tracy
CA 95376
www.thefeltedewe.com

CANADA
Yarn Canada
30-333, 28 Street NE
Calgary
AB T2A 7P4
www.yarncanada.ca

AUSTRALIA
Unicorn Fibres
Churchlands
WA 6018
www.unicornfibres.com.au

NEW ZEALAND
Ashford Store
427 West Street
Ashburton
Canterbury 7700
www.ashfordcraftshop.co.nz

Embroidery threads are easily available everywhere, however Danish Flower threads are harder to find in the U.K. and the best source is
www.danish-handcraft-guild-uk.com

about the author

Originally a children's book illustrator, Gretel was an early adopter of needle felting in 2008 when it was still a little known craft in the UK. Demonstrating her art through her blog, 'Middle of Nowhere', Gretel began selling her creations worldwide, which she continues to do today.

In 2012, she was approached by the market-leading craft magazine 'Mollie Makes' to create her first pattern, which was featured on the front cover. Gretel went on to create many more designs for 'Mollie Makes', including a further three front cover features. Her patterns have also been featured in 'Crafty', 'Craftseller' and other publications.

Gretel is now turning her skills to projects designed for crafters who want a contemporary approach to an exciting and fun craft, with patterns designed to be adaptable and inspiring.

She lives in a small cottage in rural Shropshire with three old and much loved teddy bears.

Etsy - www.etsy.com/shop/Gretelparker
Instagram - @gretelparker
Website - www.gretelparker.com
Patreon - www.patreon.com/gretelparker
Blog - www.allaroundus.blogspot.com

Acknowledgements Huge thanks to my brilliant pattern testers, Lisa Parry and Jane Smyth, for their invaluable feedback and to Katherine Raderecht and Jane Toft for their patient help and advice during the long emergence of this book.